Angus Carlyle

# A Downland Index

*Uniformbooks* 2016

First published 2016
Copyright © Angus Carlyle
ISBN 978-1-910010-10-5

*Uniformbooks*
7 Hillhead Terrace, Axminster, Devon EX13 5JL
www.uniformbooks.co.uk

Trade distribution in the UK by Central Books
www.centralbooks.com

Printed and bound by T J International, Padstow, Cornwall

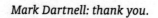

*Mark Dartnell: thank you.*

# Index

1. *It is beautiful up here. The two fields on either side present their stalks to the glow of a setting sun that still manages to let the chalk gleam. A starchy smell of the warmth that the hill has absorbed from the day; a cone of jewel-green flies hiss upwards from a drying, pitted cowpat. The crow that seems always to be here launches itself from the top rung of the fence into the stillness, its claws trailing like undercarriage. The soft report of a shotgun from the valley, then another two quickly together. A female voice from my left.*

2. *As I shut the door, three jets draw noiseless contrails southwards across the blue, each on a slightly different heading; one fuselage glints intermittently. A little later, the once sharp lines in the sky have smudged and softened, blending in with the other high cloud. Later still, tasting salt on my forearm and wincing over the flint shards, the drone of a jet lifts my head up to catch sight of a plane coming in over the Channel, its sound seems to precede it, its movement is impossibly slow, from this angle a dark cross against the now grey cloud.*

3. *At the start of the run, a small shrew, sharp snout with fine whiskers, dead on the dewy grass of the slope, the white belly fur soft to my index finger —and warm, too, either from recent life or from the already hot sun. Towards the end, above the football stadium, a rat laid out on a dry circle of blood, its face caught in a cartoon impression of a connoisseur taking a considered sniff. In between, a buzzard on the thermals, the feathers on the tips of its wings parting and shutting, a mewing cry; sudden heraldic, round-shouldered dives.*

4. *The day darkened again as I crossed into the woods from the short grass. Under the overhanging branches, the path was smooth and flat from use, winding up through open plantings of cedar, oak and beech until closed in by scrub on three sides. Looking up suddenly from watching my shoes land-ing, the silver shape that seemed to float swaying in the dim evening was only the lightness of a break in the woods set in motion by my bobbing head. The slam of a car door, three other men with their backs to me and the smell of cigarettes.*

5.  *Acid feel of vertigo crossing the curved footbridge
    over the two dual carriageways; at the apex, a
    premonition of both my hands clasping the left-
    side rail and vaulting cleanly. Past a cow with
    one horn, past the valley with the rifle range, red
    flags flapping; then, still close but higher up, to
    the memorial to the Indian war dead, a bike with
    rusted locks leaning against the fence. Sitting for a
    moment, I hear a voice: its words are indiscernible,
    yet they are as continual, as unanswered and as
    steady in register as a radio. I can see no one.*

6.  *Coming over the top of the ridge I saw the small
    herd of cows gathered around the metal gate that is
    weighted shut by a chain strung with a rusted disc
    off a plough and a rusted head of a sledge-hammer.
    The brown cows were exactly where my son and I
    had seen them three weeks ago. First one turned its
    head to me, then others, their hind legs taut, but
    none budged. I climbed one barbed wire fence and
    crawled under the next to stare down a cow blowing
    great bubbles of snot through its expanding and
    contracting nostrils.*

7.  *Swallows jink low and then up again, left then right
    over hedges full of fruit on the turn. Grouse lean
    forward and run straight, feathers matching the
    soil. I see distant shapes moving against a small
    wood; I hear them as pigs before I see them as pigs.
    Most scatter squealing as I near; the single piglet in
    the group, a clean rose hide, flattens to the ground.
    I make a wide detour over sharp stubble before
    rejoining the path and turn to see the piglet pacing
    behind me, the rest of the drove following in a quiet
    'V' formation.*

8.  *The sun is setting and my shadow elongates across
    the slope. I skirt the laden hawthorn bushes to my
    right, fearful of the blood-gorged ticks I can see
    dotting the sheep's coats. The exactness of the path's
    downward gradient suggests an engineered earth-
    work but this must be an old sheep trail, curving
    and then looping back on itself past the remains
    of the buildings the Canadians used as artillery
    targets. A lowing from across the valley gets my
    attention—so precisely typical it could have come
    from a sound effects library—some fifty cows are
    walking in steady single file.*

9. *Swishing susurrations of late summer crickets from the rubbish-strewn verge. An idea: 'Field Guide To The Roadside Weeds of Britain'. My calf muscles voice their complaints as the road stretches upwards; a small rodent crosses the path and races for the traffic-filled carriageway, its body sags in the middle like a pantomime horse whose head and tail want to go their separate ways. A blast of heat and air and noise as a silver open-top Saab veers towards me: "Run, you cunt!" The thrown cigarette butt bounces odourlessly into the cemetery wall. The passenger and driver keep their heads forward.*

10. *Tiring of tyres and engines, I cross into the woods near the old dry ski slope. A tree stump coated with white plaster, circles of blackened bricks, tarpaulins stretched out, lean-tos of rotten branches, a folded checked shirt. Now lost, I follow the twists of a shallow, narrow path. Voices somewhere and then relief to break out of the woods into a large field. A mile away, above the trees, I see the white flats near my house yet still can't place where I am nor where to go in this expanse of tufty flowerless grassland. A maze without hedges.*

11. *A golf buggy ploughs leisurely into the coarse*
    *grasses next to the Second Tee, the driver steps out*
    *in alarm, loses her footing and tumbles onto her*
    *side. Her friends rush in. Now over the fairway, my*
    *gaze guides between nettles and brambles until I*
    *catch the sudden eyes of a man to the left. All in*
    *a flash: his nose wrinkled in disdain, prone body*
    *supported by elbows and forearms behind him,*
    *striped t-shirt raised above a pale chest, ribs and*
    *scarlet nipples. A woman's clean hair covers his*
    *stomach and her face. Her floral dress. His bare feet.*

12. *Summer's last heat and we leave the wide valley,*
    *a big sky above. Gobbets of foamy saliva, a stitch*
    *starting, trying to talk about the party later. Too*
    *fast for memories: electric fences, hopping crows,*
    *the old lighthouse, tourists, up hill and down hill, up*
    *hill and down, the soft coolness in the short stretch*
    *of woods, the stiles. My friends circle at the top of*
    *the steepest slope, waiting. Out on the silvered sea,*
    *flat from this distance, a small boat returns to port.*
    *I offer an impossible wave to the fishermen, M___*
    *and D_____ wave back to me.*

13. *There is a haze up here, a haze heightened by the smears across the lenses of my glasses. Dust clouds behind a tilling tractor; pall of grey smoke rising slowly in the distant town. Tramping past the blearily watchful bull with the empty scrotum, nine crows leave nine fence posts. In the woods near the dewpond, sharp clicks of falling beech mast, pigeons' wing flaps scatter dry leaves. Squirrels scratch up trunks and scrabble between branches; one sits with bright black eyes and repeats a mantra of three croaks and one screech, with every screech its tail quivers. I'm tired.*

14. *Lightning flash and the scaffolder next door laughs. Clouds drawn from a colour strip of dark greys. Rain drums on my shoulders, drips gather on the peak of my German army cap and swing from side to side along the brim before dropping. Leaves across the wood's paths, some already rotting black. Wet lenses beneath the berries show the world upside down. 165 herring gulls on the tilled field, easier to count as I close in until they take flight like a page turned right to left. The big dead badger with the graze on its rear paw has gone.*

15. *Over the flint-coursed cemetery wall, a young
woman talks to the grave she is tending, raising her
head from weeding to gaze at the headstone. Out
at sea, a white yacht swings its mast across a patch
of brochure blue-green water whose colours are
swallowed—with the boat itself—by the shadows
from a cloudbank that trails black threads of rain.
Later, on the valley floor, the sea's cold rain sheets
through the copse I always think of as 'out-of-time'.
Two hikers sit in sodden green cagoules, hoods up,
one eats a tangerine, the other a navel orange.*

16. *A suspended bronze beech leaf is spun left and then
right. Shoes swing through wet grass; vests, shorts
and jackets swish; water sloshes from side-to-side.
Our breath: occasionally as loud and ragged rasps,
sometimes measured in and out through just-parted
lips, occasionally passing below the level of sound.
All around, a collective intimacy of wheezes, snorts,
sighs, farts and whistles, spitting and coughing.
Voices amongst friends, laughter almost until
the very end. Talk between strangers sometimes
shows that self-surprising sincerity that is born as
much from sharing a chosen hardship as it is from
knowing our ways will soon part.*

17.   *In the drizzle, the street lamps make sodium haloes
      around the crooks of the posts lining the street,
      my glasses make crosses from their light. I see my
      breath visible, I watch mist roll across the golf
      course, I follow the low-hanging clouds. Enough
      leaves in the canopy to hold off the worst of a rain
      that is now getting stronger; but the beech trunks
      have been soaked a beautiful black. I remember
      En__: "The measure of a good coffee is being able to
      taste it an hour after you've drained the cup". The
      first yellow gorse flowers are out.*

18.   *The first dewpond brims with the clearest blue sky.
      A hand dipped into the murk sends out radial ripples
      that the wind lifts into rolling bonsai waves. A
      downed parachute of a tent lies sodden over crushed
      aluminium poles. The second dewpond is filled with
      clouds that blur when I push apart the duckweed, a
      lone crow is jump-cut through the grey's undulating
      reflection. The rain sounds itself on the leaves and
      the branches and in the undergrowth a while before
      I feel any wetness. A low blackthorn bush before the
      stile tears a painless Morse cut on my shin.*

19. *I peeled apart ten layers of leaves from the path;*
    *twenty-one layers where the litterfall had been piled*
    *up by the streams of last night's storm. In the field*
    *near the dual carriageway, the grasses are dying*
    *back and snatches of sung words from a man in a*
    *smart green coat sweep in on the wind. The down-*
    *pour begins as I am peering at rash of chemical*
    *yellow mushrooms. My jacket a loose flapping sail*
    *and I run home twisted: shoulder leant into the*
    *buffeting westerly, face turned away from the rain*
    *needling cold my eye socket, cheek and forehead.*

12 NOVEMBER

20. *Mud sucks and slurps and soaks through my shoes.*
    *A reef of grey cloud peels back to leave behind a*
    *telescopic light, details shine and colours quiver.*
    *A dog walker with a red harness is circled by ten*
    *dogs. A flock of small green birds flies up: leaves in*
    *reverse. Lichen stands out here and there, I see it all*
    *around the trunks against the schoolboy/cowboy*
    *compass. High in a sycamore tree a helium balloon,*
    *once pink but now peeling to silver; once a heart but*
    *now, deflated around a branch, it is shaped like two*
    *halves of a lung.*

16 NOVEMBER

21. *Street lamps end and the darkness drops a notch.
Stars between clouds, a jet flashes, lights in straights
and curves of orange and white (and yellow when
a building closes in). Headlights send my shadow
racing out in front, sometimes a crowd of me; cars
overtake and my shadow runs past me backwards,
the grasses of the verge jagged projections; rear
lights disappear and with them any certain sense
of the path. In the city: rolling exhaust, buses lit as
hospital waiting rooms, marijuana, perfume, hot
animal protein, laughter. Tonight's harsh shout from
an idling low-slung custom car: "Bugs Bunny".*

20 NOVEMBER

22. *The leaves have chosen yellows. Yellows from the
brightest to the dullest, yellows which cast the
padlocked grit dumper in an awkward hue. On
the first loop of the woods, invisible vegetal smoke
from the allotments; on the second, something acrid
finds my nose and the surface of my eyes; on the
third, the air has drifted clear. Hawthorn berries
are darkening. Wind shells my ears, a small branch
snaps, pigeons flap, golf clubs swing metal, "Fore!,"
a single engine plane churns very low in and out of
the grey, I count 58 strides before its rumble falls
below hearing.*

23. *Around one hour after leaving home, I wake to find myself running alongside the brimming dewpond with no conscious memories of how I'd gotten there. A crow lifts itself unhurriedly over a bounding black puppy, the dog's right ear folded inside out. The paths are now slick with a mud that is too wet to hold more than the vaguest imprint of all the feet— human and animal—that have weighed down since last night. Clean-capped white mushrooms have gathered at the edge of the woods, each a toothy temptation. Sodden clothes heavy and cold, my glasses sprinkled with beads.*

24. *Out of the warm bed; out of the sleeping house. It is cold at last, cold under my fingernails and cold, later, for my feet, once the grasses have soaked through my orange shoes. The hawthorn berries are nearly black. In the woods the stripped trees now show their shapes, give the ivy a dark green moment and let the conifers in. The mud path near the witches' tree thumps hollow underfoot. Back to the emptied house, a smell of toast and lyrics abruptly attach themselves to the tune I mumbled all the way round: "Morning keep the streets empty."*

25.   *The steps in the slope that D\_\_\_\_\_, E\_ and I made are*
     *half in sun and half in shade. The blades of grass*
     *in the shade are patterned with ice, the frost made*
     *up of individual grains, each a different white. A*
     *greyhound blows a compact cloud of steam around*
     *its head. A husky has eyes of alien blue. A labrador*
     *leaps into the dewpond with a forked stick between*
     *its jaws. As the miles stretch out, my clothes get*
     *hotter and wetter, my woollen hat itching across my*
     *forehead, my lungs are drawing life in and breath-*
     *ing it out.*

26.   *After the street lamps, the heat fell with the sodium*
     *light. Winds gusted in from the west, rising near*
     *to a howl as I crossed the bridge over the dual*
     *carriageway, the wires in the fence whined a metal*
     *chorus. The moon was dented between 1 o'clock*
     *and 3 o'clock and mottled; the belt of Orion a clear*
     *stripe; red Jupiter soft above the horizon. At the*
     *same spot on the way out and on the way back, a*
     *smell of silage sharp in my nostrils and then gone.*
     *Darkness persuaded me I was running faster, as it*
     *always does.*

27.  *I pad gingerly across the paths slick with mud, my
     feet sliding the surface smooth, slipping. The leaves
     are nearly gone, the berries fallen, the grasses
     shrunk back on themselves, some wild plants still
     look strong and green under the bare hedges. Fat
     pigeon flocks crackle out of the ivy. Spots of rain and
     I am thinking clean nothing as I cross the fairway to
     re-join the woods—a blur and a growl and a prickly
     flank slams into my calves and a dog skips a circle,
     its eyes seeking mine, gums wrinkled back from its
     closed teeth, tail up.*

28.  *Blackbirds warn from tree to tree; jackdaws settle
     raucously to roost: dusk sounds for the woods. In
     the field three drones: wind rips the skeleton hedge,
     distant combustion engine smears, a jet trail chops
     in and out. Across the wet road and through the
     gap in the flint wall, with the city at my back the
     colours begin to build themselves a soft palette.
     Running home, each headlight strips away my sight,
     wobbling first at the glare and then at the black
     that follows until I remember to bend my face to the
     path. The street lamps even everything out.*

29. *I got spooked each time I approached the edge of the
woods so skirted an industrial estate and jogged
wide suburban paths until all the street lamps
had lost their orange rectangles; gulls layering
themselves in guttural, open-beaked circles above.
In among the trees at last, the gate shut that no
one had opened, the pale skin flashed that wasn't,
each snap of a twig, each flutter of feathers. At the
baker's on the way home, loaves were being neatly
arranged on the white shelves in the window, the
side door let out warmth in heat and light and smell.*

30. *Blue and white tape hung where the van crashed;
yellow and black tape twisted near the sparse
branches whose few leaves show pink; short strips
of red and white tape were each weighed down by a
flint near the wall whose repair had stalled. The old
paths were churned to ridges of mud and craters of
rainwater and the backs of my shoes were sucked
noisily away from my heels. New paths were already
being begun, the grasses bent darker where fresh
feet trod, different paws pressed and other wheels
turned. A hollow trunk was deep enough to climb
inside.*

31.  *Smoke struggles from a chimney; mist hangs in only
     one part of the valley. Ice sheets across the second
     dewpond and three half-moons: chalk against blue,
     yolk against purple, silver against blue-black. A
     larger animal stops moving in the undergrowth
     when I stop jogging and dusk fears descend again.
     Away from the unfamiliar path—dodging trees and
     hitting trees—I send crows out of their roosts before
     me in feathery, hoarse complaint. A half-minute later,
     is this the same horde that has just settled onto new
     perches or are they different birds that rise loudly
     into the quiet?*

32.  *The air was thin and blue and still. My left knee
     was throbbing before the watch beeped us past the
     first mile. From the bridge to the traffic island and
     then gingerly over the mire where the brambles
     got cut back. (The black and white 'HMS Pinafore'
     record sleeve is still wedged high in the branches).
     Freddy is on the lead when I slip on the hill where
     the sheep have been grazing; he is bounding—both
     shaggy forepaws off the ground—among the thin
     sycamores to our right when M___ stubs his toe on
     a tree root.*

33. *Wind rattles the treetops like a recording. A branch falls onto the path and sends up a spray of mud, muddy water and soft splinters of wood. A crow makes stretching strides and pigeons explode from bushes and hedges, compressed detonations of feathers, foliage and rainwater. I am squelching, slithering and mincing. I catch myself imagining imminent injuries. Passing a pile of Christmas trees, I hear a lamppost imitate a yacht mast (only the second time this). Gusts barrel into me, shoving me forward or sending me sideways, my German army cap flies off and under a passing prison van.*

34. *The starlings have gathered on the radio mast. All up the taut diagonal guy-wires, all along the lateral struts, all over the metal diamonds of the structure's shaft; perched on concave dishes, oblong boxes, aerials and wind vanes, the rungs of the ladder and the triangles that top the surrounding fence. Their fizzing, clicking and crackling can be heard from the other side of the road. Closing one finger for every ten I count and remembering each hundred made by two closed fists, I blow steam until I reach a thousand birds. Returning an hour later, the mast stands bare.*

35. *The sun is strobed through the trees—a rural dream machine—by my running up the path. A splayed, gloved hand's width from the southern horizon, the sun is visible through the cloud as a duller disk fringed with fluorescence. The sun sends light to brighten the bark of a downed beech tree, to pick out wet hummocks of moss, to mirror the bare branches in shallow puddles, to show the last patches of snow. (I remember this morning before dawn watching spots of snow fall slowly, quietly. A dirty-tailed fox daintily sharing the pavement and cocking its small head).*

36. *A short-haired dog licks at the ground, stretching its jaws and shifting its head to seek the best contact for its pink and white tongue. An unconcerned magpie rides a thin branch an arm's length away, enamel green and beetle blue on its flank; sickle moon the top of a toe-nail. Out in the open, leaves blown onto the trails have alchemised to mud; under the shelter of trees they still hold some shape and colour. I jump a curve of barbed wire, I smell a campfire, I see a purple tent, I feel sadness come like a sudden shower.*

37.  *On the trails beneath some of the trees, in the lee of
     some hedges, there are still delicate archipelagos of
     snow. On the fairways, small wedges of ice crystals,
     often tilted and moulded to the curve of a boot heel
     or toe, track the early morning walkers. A shadow of
     a small bird flits between the shadows of branches
     and I find a small ball of lichen of such a green and
     such a shape that I think of plastic bags filled with
     railway modeller's foliage. I carry it in the palm of
     my hand where it shrinks and darkens.*

38.  *Miniature flakes of snow fall to dust the rigid paths
     silver; the ice on the first dewpond is not yet strong
     enough to bear my weight. A chalk swastika on
     one tree trunk and "RAC LIV SAM MAX" on the
     next. I turn back, spit on my fingers and rub out the
     swastika; my palm still smells sour an hour later. I
     meet a man who claims to be the city's last shrimp
     fisherman to use a hand net; the handle of his crutch
     wrapped in perishing rubber bands, he tells me of
     romantic adventures in Finland 50 years ago.*

39. *The wind is so brutal that I am laughing: it rips the steam from my mouth, brings tears to the corners of my eyes, claims my spit before the ground, stings the tips of my ears and has my bare hands mottled white and red. The wind shoves and pushes, seems to breeze from every direction, as strong on the slopes as on the crests of our little hills. The wind whines and rattles at my jacket, alternately smoothing the fabric to my skin then dragging it away. The sky darker at the velodrome, I notice the air has stilled.*

40. *In the first seconds of the door shutting: four soft wing beats from a gull five feet above, two clicks from a starling, a magpie's rattle, a blue tit's phrase and three caws from a crow straining from a roof ridge opposite. The late afternoons have (suddenly) found more time. Snowdrops in small clusters— hoods still closed—tiny violets hidden in the dead hedge and buds on some branches' tips and edges. Wetness suspended in the air. The sky was an undifferentiated grey until, passing the phone mast, I saw beams break the clouds and spot-light the sea silver.*

41. *The sky to the east is thick with cloud shading towards black; to the west patches of blue break thinner white reefs. Close to the sea, two stripes from the sun strike like searchlights; nearer still and now five spots aim down at the surf. Twenty gulls circle grey without flapping; waves rear to three metres before hurling onto the shingle; salt on my lips, sulphide sharp in my nostrils. Spume has bloomed along the shore—on the beach and on the promenade—gritty to touch. Legs wobbling on the final hill; I'm spitting white, nose running clear.*

42. *Afternoon into evening, my shadow grows longer and shorter, thinner and fatter. From the highest point, I can count the smoke from fourteen bonfires; next to the chalk path, there are sheep climbing rotting bales of straw. Heading back, the patch of red where the sun once was gets slowly squashed to nothing and the horizon becomes bars of dark greys, of purples and of sulphur's yellows. When I drop from the ridge into a valley, the temperature drops with me. Dark shapes detach from trees and there is an owl or a shout. My shadows return with the headlights.*

43.   *High clouds stretch from the land out across the sea,*
      *curving in bands grooved by blue sky. Sounds hang*
      *soft in the stillness. And even less: my feet strike the*
      *gravel and the low sun lights the hair on the left*
      *of my legs; my fists bring the faintest smell of soap*
      *when they wind towards my face; my knees still*
      *sting inside from time to time; my mouth (caught*
      *off-guard) grunts with animal strain or opens to an*
      *'O'; my motor-body's actions phase in and out; my*
      *perceptions oscillate on and off; my thoughts flicker*
      *between full and empty.*

44.   *I feel the gravel through my soles, feel where stones*
      *have built up and where they have worn away, feel*
      *my toes splaying and squashing, feel the ridges of*
      *bone on the top of my feet, feel my ankles falling,*
      *twisting and rising. Concentrating so closely but*
      *still my heels land first. The sun's ember leaves an*
      *orange sheen along flat roofs, across windows and*
      *inside puddles, the orange almost matches the glow*
      *the street lamps are beginning to offer. A man in a*
      *green jumper, grey tracksuit bottoms and a black*
      *watch cap eases alongside and then quickly past.*

45.  *Later on I grasp that the world's colours have dulled down. Before any wetness registers on my shorn head, I see rain dropping on the packed earth, see it on the exposed chalk and flint, see it bead the fence, see it thread the air. Darker and cold enough for a vigorous hail to drum itself out and leave slow, soggy snowflakes. My legs feel the heat from the traffic. Where the three boys had huddled when I left the house is now a litter of balloons and shiny metal cylinders. The parked cars are patterned with paisleys of ice.*

46.  *A hospital crutch—chrome shaft and grey plastic handle—is rammed deep into a bank of earth to wedge a wooden pallet against a fence. A holly bush has been ripped out of the ground and flattened. The mist closes things down: 100 metres in our street, 50 metres near the school, 20 metres at the top of the first hill: silhouettes of grey slowly acquire colour (red hat, white bag, brown Shetland pony). If I plan, I run slower; if I dream, I run slower still; if I think body (think muscles, joints, lungs, heart, spine) I speed up.*

47. *Blue sky with clumps of Rorschach cloud: a crying child, a lantern, a scorpion, an island, a hammock, some pliers. A row of flowers on the verge with petals in shades of washed-out violet, my thighs stiffen when I straighten myself again. A further distance opens up; shadows scud over interlocking hills and, through the gaps between their brown flanks, glimpses of more remote geology. The sweat on my scalp and in my eyebrows, the wet in my beard and the dampness on the small of my back all dry off when I turn into the wind; hot becomes cold.*

48. *A buzzard hangs in the wind above the woods before folding out of sight. The day grows dimmer and then brighter as banks of cloud gather then part. When the light darkens, the temperature seems to drop and the wind seems to rise— chopping the skylark's song, rattling the scrubby bushes, bending the taller trees. For the last two miles, smell leads me home (though this, too, is swept in and out): damp hay, fires from caravans, from allotments and from household hearths, roasting dinners. I begin to wonder if my new shorts are cut for a woman's shape.*

49. *First circle: jogging up the valley, birds dip chirrup-*
    *ing under fences, warble hidden in hedges and flute*
    *from leafless perches to surround me on every side*
    *and from every height. So much song is pouring out*
    *of so many open beaks that the whole scene edges*
    *towards excess. Second circle: breathing hard over*
    *the old estate paths, eight dogs and their teeth ring*
    *around me, yelping, growling, snarling and barking*
    *hoarse. The sheerness of this scene borders on a*
    *kind of caricature (utopian animal eternities from*
    *old Watchtower covers but also the onomatopoeia*
    *invoked by the "friends of last evening").*

50. *The land is catching its breath. That uprooted*
    *holly was bound flat by a sharp bramble cord; the*
    *crutch continues to wedge against the fence; trees*
    *remain bare and most leaves have dissolved into*
    *mud. Mushrooms—yellow or clean—are no longer*
    *around; the striped tape has disappeared; the 'HMS*
    *Pinafore' album is faded and buckled and has fallen*
    *to the ground; the three dewponds are brimming;*
    *the cows are not back in the field with the metal*
    *gate. The copse still feels as if out-of-time; I still get*
    *vertigo over the bridges; dusk can still make me*
    *shudder.*

51. *Morning: clouds congregating and then drifting apart; winds raising the motion of leaves from the mutest shiver into churning waves that roll from one tree to the next until exhausted. Afternoon: everything clears in calm air for the sun to take hold and for heat, light and blue to follow us into dusk. If it always feels that there is always one day when a season clicks into the next, then today is that day. Against our flow: glints catching glasses outside pubs, smiles across the shingle, cars jamming junctions, friends holding the pavement width and soap in their wake.*

52. *Goose flesh rises across my thighs as I open the door to a mottled grey-white threaded with darker bands. At the old estate wall, a tractor almost obscured by its trefoil cargo of round hay bales swings right and into the ruts behind me. At the bottom of the narrow sloped track leading out of the woods I see a couple in woollens and fleeces twisted into an oblivious embrace. My face averted for as much of the minute it takes me to finally reach them as possible, they are still eyes shut, pawing and kissing as I sidle past.*

53.   *Colder. Greyer. Starlings launch off the car show-room roof in fits and starts. They swirl out into an almost-pattern for a slowly murmured count of ten, twelve or seventeen then settle for a few moments of whirring and ticking before rising up again. The 400 or so birds keep at this interrupted calligraphy for over an hour and then disperse. A collarless dog with a patch of black fur over its eye; the mist releases the finest spray of droplets; a runner screams past with even shorter shorts than mine, his calves dense with tattoos; a friend beeps a greeting.*

54.   *The paths are decorated with tree shadows, intricate across the homemade bike trails. A bonfire bubbles the air, growls and cracks. A sudden grin on my mouth and in my eyes. Everyone out in the sun of the village's single street: a hired gardener chats to someone weeding their own borders; a map passed noisily between a local and a hiker; dog walkers tangle their leads; three kids—vaping—peer at a horse chewing a fence post; a woman sits on a folded newspaper, her shoes neatly off, basking. This year's first freckles have appeared where my hairline has receded.*

55. *Sour in my mouth: something of last night's Red Stripe mixed with the aftertastes of this morning's espresso, toothpaste, spinach juice and cod liver oil. A sharpness where my throat meets my neck. Early clouds bunch high above the shoreline and separate into wider and wider bands as I move inland. Buds on different trees seem to be colouring green, red and yellow from their insides to their outsides. On my own until two sweat-soaked runners materialise from the second wood. I hear "like a rabbits" offered with a smile. A puzzle until I sneak back into the waking house.*

56. *On our route down to the coast, I see the first sprays of pink and white blossom. The wind blows from east to west along the promenade and—for all its size—the sea seems somehow subdued. Gulls' feathers shade from blacks to greys to vivid silvers as they angle in the changing light. Runners of every age are out in early force: stooped with exertion, full of beans, patched with sweat stains, stumbling, at full stretch, alone, heads turned in calm conversation, with dogs trotting and bounding, in vests, in cagoules, with opened senses and with narrowed focus.*

57.   *Across the road, a man in his early twenties, head
      recently shaved, kneels and convulses through waves
      of reddish vomit. His friend strums a battered guitar.
      An ash-coloured bowl has been turned upside down
      to seal the earth in an almost uniform expanse.
      Where the haloed sun pushes through the grey, the
      clouds take distinct shapes, appear darker and in
      motion. I squint into the glare and shield my eyes
      with an untidy salute. A magpie hangs upside down
      to tear off a twig; two jays screech two undulating
      flights; fourteen sparrows feed in a brown bush,
      synthesising avian FX.*

58.   *Shivering in a tent before the start among close
      warm bodies and smells of vapour rub. We had
      bumped into "like a rabbits" on the early train and
      see them at the finish, wet as sandbags and beaming
      hot. Gloves, jackets, jumpers, bin bag tabards, gel
      packets and water bottles discarded along the route;
      I select and hunt 'frenemies'; I calculate fractions;
      I repeat homespun mantras; I check my thirst, my
      bladder, my bowels and my watch (check that a lot);
      I only speak to two other runners and only absorb
      fragments of the crowd, the buildings or the sky.*

59.  *In a suntrap against the station wall, the bees
     busying in and out of the pink blossom are hard to
     separate from their shadows. Open-sided industrial
     barns filled with grey rubble and scrap—two freshly
     painted stock cars, radio voices—lead to a small
     park, pungent green of nettles and cow-parsley,
     and then to the raised river bank that will meander
     eight miles north. The tidal river flowing upstream,
     currents sliding and curling: a cormorant warms its
     prehistoric plumage, a heron drifts over the reeds,
     the cries of new-born lambs, hidden behind the
     opposite bank, carry clear across the water.*

60.  *The black and white feathers flashed across the path
     to shift from a fleeting sense of magpie by shrink-
     ing, speeding up, stuttering their flight and shaping
     themselves a red cap to land as a woodpecker on the
     beech trunk and claw upwards in slow, scratching
     spirals. The trails have dried out and hardened,
     the branches and twigs on the shrubs and trees are
     speckled with growing green. Six yellow flowers:
     there's the furze after all these months but now
     dandelion, wild daffodil, buttercup, ragwort and
     celandine. A motionlessness that is not just a lack
     of wind: something stalling, suspended, still.*

61. *A plastic doll's house door in cartoon green lay on the scuffed cinder path. There was a softening of shape and subduing of sound that I wanted to call 'submarine' but I think that word came more from my struggles to push one knee in front of the other, to drag my feet off the ground, to overcome heavy limbs and feeble muscles, the desire today just to sink down, curl up and close my eyes. It's only when heading down our street and Mi___ calls something I can't make out that I hear I have been muttering to myself.*

62. *The third dewpond mirrors swaying trees, the blue sky above them and two columns of black smoke rising from disposable barbecue trays. Five picnickers stand back, the women in high-heeled shoes and patterned dresses nipped at their waists, the men's hair crisp partings and recently shortened back and sides. Staccato clicks when the uppermost twigs collide in the breeze, scraping from lower branches and groans from the rubbing of bifurcated trunks. On the curving path leading to the stile and the stunted blackthorn, columns of waxy ivy glint shimmering silver as the wind angles the leaves to the setting sun.*

63. *Compacted chalk inclined towards the gate, banked above the cars. Curving, rising sheep track, tilted to the valley bowl below. Breaching, twisting roots from tiny tendrils to shoulder socket size. Green splaying shoots through coarse soil scattered with thin flints. Broken beech burrs, spatterings of bird shit, ground compressed flat. Cinder scuffed over the camber by skidding wheels and feet. Grey paving slabs play Tetris with different shades of pink. Loose shards of broken bottles sprinkle the dark glass-mixed asphalt. The pavement bulges over the elm roots; kids' chalk hieroglyphs. Hot blue sky above, rain squeezed out of the air.*

64. *A slight, dun-coloured bird skips once, twice and then a third time before dropping into the sea wall's shadow and emerging with a fat moth clamped in its beak. Black smoke billows up through the shimmer over the city. I look back again and the plume has almost cleared, dark diagonal trails head away from the shore. Waves send the pebbles ringing, waves lap delicately, waves trundle a boulder up and down the steps of a slipway, waves crash and shoot spray. Bending to fill my camouflage cap with seawater, a carpet of white foam rushes cold over my ankles.*

65. *The light before breakfast picks out every colour. It sharpens bricks and mortar, tiles, blossom, leaves, feathers, grass stalks, tarmac, parked cars, telephone wires and poles, cat fur, clothing, skin and hair, glasses, eyes and jewellery, the flanks of horses, slides in playgrounds, the gravestones stacked in the stonemasons and the gravestones in the flint-walled cemetery, fence posts and fence wire. The light glares in windows, glitters the sea's surface, dazzles the chalk cliffs (fulmars gurgle from their holes). September's silver Saab is negated by a black BMW convertible whose driver beeps encouragement and waves me up the same hill.*

66. *Daffodils droop leached yellow; dandelions have sent up clocks. I suck on the flower of a white deadnettle but can't taste the honey of my childhood woods. I yawn and my jaw cracks out of joint. I cradle the jowl in my right palm for a few steps, thumb follows my jawline, fingers hold the lobe from front and behind, curl over the tragus and touch the smooth flesh next to my eye socket. Early grey morning. I watch a magpie dismantle twigs from one nest and reassemble them in another high in the tree opposite. I think about stopping.*

67.  *Shins feel sharp and shoulders stiff; eyes bulge
     with a hangover. Large out of its sky and larger
     fanning its bright wings, a seagull tears at a burnt
     corncob. Late, I wave an apology to G____ and
     we set off through the streets. At the park, the
     loudhailer starts everyone going: all shapes and all
     sizes, bunched together and spread apart, friends,
     children and parents, people alone, dogs and
     prams. From the sidelines: counting out minutes
     and seconds, quiet cheers, rattles and names. After
     the finish: some talk, some lean in silence, some
     turn to clap the next ones home.*

68.  *Today I am typing: wind below breath, wooden
     table warm to the touch, sky a hard blue. Yesterday
     I was running: low cloud swallowed seagulls and
     pulled the world in tight, gutters overflowed to pour
     cold rods, breeze swept through a sticky confetti
     of pink blossom, white blossom and green flakes of
     elm scored with scarlet. Slugs and snails, crushed
     and intact. Bluebells bowed down, wet smells of
     scythed parsley, grass and nettles. A brown jowly
     dog coughed behind a wall then padded painfully
     through a gap, its rear legs parted by a distended
     growth hanging almost to the ground.*

69. *Waddling down the stairs, gripping the bannister, stiff thighs and sore across my lower back. A glass of water and I'm remembering: crow blown backwards, raising and lowering its wings for stability (flight in reverse); furze at its most yellow; alternating bands of brightness and cloud shadows racing up the valley-side (timelapse without the camera); lamb flanks sprayed with numbers (158, 108); cackling at the ferocious wind (lifting from behind, heaving sidewards, almost stopping me in my tracks, roaring trees like surf); calm shelter of the out-of-time copse (every green out there and a fresh entrance for the badger sett).*

70. *Yeah, Hi. Hello. Hi. Out late! Morning. Hi. Sorry. Hi. Hi. Thanks. Why do we do this, eh? Morning. Morning. Soaked. You're working hard! Hello. Still at it? Hiya. Beautiful day, we're so lucky. Morning. They won't bite! Morning. Oh, Hi. Excuse me, Mister; excuse me? Hi. Hi. Are you going on Saturday? Evening. Hi. You must be mad at this time of night. Hello. Hiya. Hi. Hi. Come through. Cheers. See you later. I won't shake your hand. How far you going? Hello. Hi. You running to vote? Hello. All right? Leave it open, please. Hi. Good evening. Hi.*

71.  From the accelerating train I catch a glimpse of
     yesterday's streets. I recall the first faint sugges-
     tions of moisture on my lower leg hairs; later, more
     substantial drips (more puzzling); and then the real-
     isation that my leaking backpack water bladder had
     drenched my shorts. The first schoolboy prodded his
     right middle finger into my belly, made a popping
     sound and a hiss of deflation. The fourth boy gyrated
     his hips and sung, in tune, "I'm sexy and I know
     it". The fifth faltered, pointed and shouted—almost
     more in horror than in mockery—"My God, he's
     pissed himself!"

72.  Last night I woke with a start when the train jolted
     to a halt. A little woozy and lent a limp by cramp,
     I cradled my rucksack and jacket and hobbled onto
     the platform. I gingerly pulled on my running gear
     in a station toilet cubicle. The warning light on
     top of a crane a bright red star. A soft whirlwind
     of elm blossom in the headlights. Shoulders back,
     stomach clenched and speeding up for every Friday
     pub crowd, cigarette squints, white-toothed smiles,
     sudden fireworks, chair scrapes, everyone leaning
     together, everyone happy. Wanting to get home,
     wanting to keep running.

19 MAY

73. *I feel sweat: drying to salt crinkling my brow,
    damp between shoulder blades, moist on these
    typing fingertips. Thinking back to the sweet
    tang from swaying stretches of parsley (brushing
    their now-white heads passed on tiny flowers and
    unexpected amounts of water); taste of tin on my
    lips and a sensation like battery contacts for my
    tongue; sun starting to rise behind white cloud,
    glistening liquorice slugs, a pair of mallards jerked
    close through synchronised changes of direction.
    Worrying about making it to work on time as I
    touched the lamppost and worrying again now,
    breathing in the bright kitchen.*

21 MAY

74. *Growing growls of traffic push past the just-opened
    window to weaken my memory's hold on the first
    hush of the street. Bluebell haze. The shelters being
    hidden away until their Autumn return. The far
    knuckles of land smooth and green, spotted in
    their folds by darker and rougher patches of trees.
    Running shadow right at my side heading north,
    edging further in front on the way south. The dull
    navy sea between the city valley's shallow sides
    distorts into a distant range, foothills for a Fuji of
    white cloud. Stretching for her cereals, my daughter
    asks, "What are you writing?"*

75. *I can recall that six days ago, I: tasted the copper
coin on my tongue and at the roof of my mouth;
noticed the green of the trees shading into brown at
their crowns; saw squirts of purple bird droppings;
heard the raucous start of the holidays; looked from
a fresh angle at the slope with the third dewpond;
felt the stones of the new path sharp under my soles;
regretted going out for so long without any food.
Thinking back, I cannot recall: the colour of the
sky, whether it was warm or cool or what we talked
about.*

76. *Sausage fingers, sunburnt neck, right nipple raw
from the strap of my new water bladder. These are
immediate: the black-haired, pale-skinned arse of the
angler squatting on the towpath, orange hi-vis vests
under the bridge and to the east on the Miyazaki
railway line, the looming CGI incinerator, the goose's
wing muscles, skidding swans' feet, a dainty egret,
frogs somehow both tired and energetic, purple-
painted stock car, waving to the father and son
in their inflatable canoe, heron circling large. The
repeated impression that the opposite riverbank was
moving in one direction and the round hills behind
moving in another.*

77. *Polished blues above. The vine's splaying leaves are getting ruffled by a breeze that comes and goes with too little force to interrupt the hanging, circling and zigzagging compositions of the hoverflies that I can see through the window. Last night's sky had brought the wind right up and dropped dark clouds down low. Rain poured exhilaration to overflow the drains, to race miniature rivers down the gutters, to sheet leaves and litter down the pavements, to soak my camo cap in seconds, to flood the crossroads as high as our shins, to send skirts of water flaring from cars.*

78. *Striding off the empty platform, hands flicking ostentation from wrists, hands fiddling intently at the water bladder, hands palming each knee in turn until—after a surreptitious scan reveals no potential audience—I settle into an unfussy jog that takes me across the stone bridge above the stream's fish and waving weeds, through the flinted and thatched village, over the first stile (its lowest rung smeared with dog shit freshly scraped from a shoe) and up onto the escarpment where I murmur to scattering sheep, find drifting wet mists and another out-of-time knot of hill, tree and sky.*

79. *Suddenly hot after the sudden downpour, pavements
steam as if newly-laid. My nostrils open to a biscuity
petrichor aroma (as they open later when muggy
greens evaporate off the seeding grasses). The water
in my bottle warms, my forehead crinkles with salt,
the netting in these shorts chafes. Up the long hill
I shake off a premonition that I am going to tip
backwards and tumble; I am heartened by a happy,
sweeping "Ahoy!" from another runner, teeth smiling
bright in his red face, belly like a basketball below a
flat chest that sprouts an unruly clump of white hair.*

80. *A punctured moon rose pink behind a cliff of cloud.
Lightness lingered above but was draining grittily
away below. In the deepening dusk, wildflowers lost
their colours, the whites of the ox-eye daisies the
last to be let go. Back to the city under a startling
red sky: onto the steep, long, downward hill and:
really running, shortening strides, running leaning
forward, running laughing, skidding off the pavement—knee buckling then righting—out to the
white lines of the road, running squeezed between
hot moving cars, their lights, horns and gestures
and wolf whistles from the smokers outside the pub.*

81. *Young seagulls whistled between chimney pots,*
    *soaring older birds tendered abrasive, percussive*
    *'chugs' or screams that stretched out then choked to*
    *a stop. Sunshine had jammed the roads with idling*
    *engines and filled the pavements with crowds to*
    *weave our way through. I peeled my vest over my*
    *head while the pebbles slipped and grated at each*
    *step; I bent down to shuck my feet out of my shoes*
    *and hook my socks off my feet; I stumbled, steadied*
    *and launched through the waves and under, eyes*
    *open for greens and yellows and whites and the skin*
    *of my arms.*

82. *The cinder path is hemmed-in by an extravagance*
    *of wildflowers: bindweed has sent out white papery*
    *trumpets, ragwort clusters yellow, teasels rise*
    *over my shoulders, poppies droop and drop petals,*
    *nettles and Queen Anne's Lace find a second wind,*
    *red clover sways. The squat pylon at the crossroads*
    *in the woods fizzed like hot wet fat and hummed.*
    *On the athletics track, nine kites string ribbons*
    *in their wake, a bouncy castle sags and a group*
    *of picnickers clutching bottles stagger from their*
    *blankets to offer me ironic cheers as I struggle up*
    *the steep hill back into the woods.*

83.   *I've remembered to remember: the desiccated rat,
      the wary dog chained to the caravan, the electric
      crickets pulsing from the undergrowth, the stripes
      of clouds curving to tails, me mulling over why
      everyone at the pub finds my anecdotes boring, the
      runner who blanks an early morning greeting, the
      warmth of the air that stretches my nostrils. Typing
      this out on the train into work, all other detail has
      evaporated, leaving me with a familiar route, my
      usual outfit, the key slipped from my back pocket,
      the door that opened to quietness, shoes off and
      padding up the carpeted stairs.*

84.   *On the new path, a crow with a broken wing splays
      hopping before me, cawing furiously. Above the
      out-of-time copse, the gorse have lost their flowers
      but found something special: cobwebs stretch
      between thorns as balls, as pyramids, as hammocks,
      as canopies and these geometries glitter: pinprick
      beads gather near drops the size of tears. The mist
      at the high ridge—scudded by a sharp wind—draws
      visibility in below twenty metres and sheep startle
      and twist away, thumping the ground as I call out
      to calm them. Near a restaurant in the town, smells
      of burnt garlic.*

85.  *The wildflowers have been cut back roughly: sodden*
     *stalks, dulled petals, crumbling flower heads, scat-*
     *tered leaves and decapitated thistle crowns strewn*
     *across the path. I am panting between sentences*
     *on the straights, between phrases as the hill starts*
     *to rise, down to single words as the steepness bites*
     *and then head dropped and wordless as Mill Road*
     *stretches on. Rounding the final corner I see M___*
     *already alternating squats and stretches with*
     *jogging round in circles. I reward myself with a*
     *homemade snack unwrapped from tinfoil. The low*
     *grey sky's rain poured coldness: soaking all the way*
     *through in seconds.*

86.  *The corn swayed from the two fields on either side,*
     *stalks shorter than they were twelve months ago*
     *and duller in a light that has closed over again after*
     *the brief brightness that pricked my neck with heat.*
     *Running left for the first time from the gate weighed*
     *shut by a log suspended on frayed blue 12-ply farm*
     *twine, the spot-lit sea to the south, a plain chequered*
     *by field, hedge and settlements to the north. The*
     *ridge rises tough and falls tougher, all my weight to*
     *the top of my knees, flints stabbing my soles, feeling*
     *my heart throb.*

87. *In the field to the right, dirty-wooled sheep have settled into a jagged arrowhead formation from which sprout rain-darkened shrubs that I have never noticed before. In the field over the cinder track—the pallet lying crutchless—brighter-coated sheep drum the tight earth in a chase for the shepherd. Only yellow ragwort constellations and white bindweed trumpets and the realisation that no bird sings or calls. As the sky clears, I pass "like a rabbits" heading into the woods. Both have surprisingly developed upper arms; the woman cups her mouth to call and remind me of the funeral.*

88. *At the incinerator above the railway bridge the heat is already slicking arms with sweat and roughening the breath. The stones of the new path were spread with a smooth glistening black that clutched at my soles, diverting me into the stubble, where the sliced stalks scratched a discomfort I remember from thirty-five years ago. Even hotter in the valley bowl beyond the out-of-time copse, the nature reserve's steep chalks, flints and packed earth shimmered with a hallucination of tiny butterflies, clouds of soft greys, blues and whites opening and closing at my feet, climbing a few inches and dropping.*

89.   *The weekend's downpours have transformed the*
*paths into museum dioramas: scaled-down gullies*
*and canyon strata on the cinder path, river deltas in*
*the second wood and a battlefield's flooded craters*
*in the third. Murky bands of rain sweep across the*
*western hillsides while to the east patches of cloud*
*are pearlised by the hidden sun. Clover, heather and*
*thistle, flat mushrooms and rounded ones, pristine*
*and tattered; in the second and fourth dewponds,*
*grasses sway in the water. From a group of drookit*
*hikers more ironic wolf whistles, I turn laughing and*
*spot a clothes peg pinned to my shorts.*

90.   *Dirt in the drained bath; opened the door to dinner's*
*smell; 73 starlings fizzed the phone mast; nagging*
*myself for raising a middle finger to the scowling*
*runner's back; slipped on the chalk sheets near the*
*stile; crows hunched and launched into the gale; fist*
*made tinfoil asteroid; smoke 'V' from distant fire;*
*mist in the trees in lee of the ridge; bright patches*
*of sun on the plain; grunts, groans and sighs;*
*commentary out loud for the glimpse of beauty at*
*the curving, rising sheep track; everything blurred*
*without glasses; elated by the rain; closed the door*
*behind me.*

91. *Two buzzards slide over the southern face of the woods then slip beneath the overlapping screens of leaves that have just started to turn. Shadows hatch depth into the distance; sunlight shines stalks of grass and draws out scarlets in hawthorn, rosehip and holly. The honk of a pheasant in the valley bowl, the grating of a car's gears near the second dewpond—sound is wrapped in a protective bubble, its details prolonged. Avoiding eye contact, humming, I mince past the cows stretched out in the clover. One hauls upright, tosses its head and kicks hind hooves in the air.*

92. *Orange, dented and falling through the trees on the left and then below the ones to my right; yellow between the rows of terraced houses; white under tracking cloud: three more moons. A single cricket throbs at the flint wall. The head torch magnifies each spray of spit and picks out a swirling cloud of scattered dots in front of my face. The nearest tree trunks seem to bend into the glowing circle out of a grainy darkness. My breath rasping, each beech mast caught underfoot cracking, soles thump, sweating, wind rushes the leaves and I find a fear again.*

93.   *Two white butterflies rose spinning together over
      the parked cars. Two cormorants perched on two
      outflow pipes. The lock swung open for a yacht. An
      urban dream machine: sun pulsed through the metal
      security fence, chromatic clouds for my squinting
      eyes. Two swans drifted over the flooded grasses at
      the edge of the lagoon. Two men—their bodies in
      shade, their faces golden—smooched in the fishing
      boat beached on breeze blocks, mouths working, one
      clasping the back of the other's head. My backpack
      drained, no drop to be wrung from the bladder,
      I start walking. Crooked exhausted smile.*

94.   *Yellow leaves drop from the trees and crackle under
      my soles. Smells of hearths and bonfires. Orange
      leaves, horse chestnuts and beech, swish from my
      toes. A crow hops off the low slope and sashays
      onto the park; skewered on its beak is a large apple,
      almost intact but with some peel nibbled away. The
      undergrowth near the fence is wilting and turning
      brown. A tight flock of pigeons—some glide as
      fleurs de lys—twist and tumble past the mobile
      phone mast. At the flint wall, the weeds are still
      green. Leg muscles heavy and the skyline soft.*

95.   *Streaks of red and purple above the valley bowl and
      I am a sundial for my shadow. A bleached moon is
      feathered behind cloud; mist pools the lower slopes
      and probes the treeline (I pull my glasses off to clean
      them and feel cobwebs stuck to my face, hair and
      beard). In the grainy dusk, the woods have black
      blobs for entrances and white blobs for exits; the
      soft green blobs are retinal echoes from the pulsing
      light on my vest. An owl's hoot and the moon has
      shrugged off its shroud to cast sharp shadows and
      ghost the contrails.*

96.   *Moths shimmer in the beam, breath clouds sparkle,
      a bat flickers near the hedge and I'm crossing the
      field, the cows' eyes glow, a steady circle shifts to
      two gleaming hemispheres (a flash of something
      twisted inside), first one cow lows, then another,
      hooves scrape stiff grasses, louder moans, snorts,
      thumps of momentum and my torch is off, arms
      slashing, stumbling sightless down the valley, legs
      twisting and slipping, feet skating across cowpats,
      toes stubbing flints and climbing the steep far
      slope, staggering between gorse bushes to the gate,
      fumbling the catch and pushing through, leaning
      back, grinning, rasping, sweating.*

97.   *Leap, splash and skirt the milky tea puddles up
      to the ridge: height lets in the distance and how
      things connect. "The light is falling." Leaning down
      the long curving slope, reverberating the stone
      archway below the train track, following the dual
      carriageway back to the city (I wince and grate my
      teeth at the shrieking nearside lane and the thicker,
      lower, jagged tearing from the further lane; fumes
      in my throat and eyes). The sun squashes scarlet
      below the horizon and the skin above my right sock
      is warmed briefly as it slices through a cairn of
      horse dung.*

98.   *Above the far rim of the valley bowl, the fences on
      either side of the chalk path rise into a mist that
      opens and closes, letting shapes loom, find detail
      and then dissolve: ramblers and runners, the big bull,
      a cow scratching its ear with a hind leg, the damp
      green of clover, the yellow of hawkbit and the purple
      of a vetch, another bronze beech leaf spinning, the
      fourth dewpond strobed out of greyness by camera
      flashes. When I turn for home, the villages down on
      the plain glow in the blue dark like oilrigs seen from
      an aircraft.*

99. *Eyes fixing on mine, a dog walker cupped my left elbow in his palm and said, "That rotten branch fell like a dead body. Straight down. Right down". Leaving him with the branch, I trotted through the wind-roared woods: saw a blue and green tent protected by a crude lean-to, heard an electricity pole sputter and thrum and felt a shower of sideways rain. 3 buzzards showed their feather details near the out-of-time copse, 7 magpies left a bare tree at its entrance, 47 crows strutted the hill above the sett, 14 grouse exploded out of the valley bowl field.*

100. *It is still beautiful up here. A cold foul rain gusts from every side, toes wet in mud-coated shoes, throbbing right knee, aching lower back. The low dark sky has pulled the land in tight: blackened cow parsley, dripping fence squares, shards of flint, lumps of chalk, puddles and grasses, rolled waves of ploughed soil to the left, new shoots to the right, the watchful cows drenched. A mile more along the ridge and—turning from closing the farm-twine-gate—I am stopped by a rainbow of five hikers on their way down from the Beacon: laughter is our recognition.*

# *Outro*

"The facts speak for themselves (and the list is not exhaustive)"
—Jean-François Lyotard, *The Postmodern Condition* (1979).

The Beacon is a high point on the low crease of land that I have been running along. It is a spindle around which revolve the valley bowls, the fields left to grass and clover and the fields ploughed and tilled (with shoots in the spring and stubble in the late summer), the four dewponds, the roads, tracks, trails, paths, railway lines and bridges, the out-of-time copse, the woods at dusk and dawn, the stream and the river, the hedges and incinerators, the plains to the north with rising bonfire smoke and to the south, the sea with its moods and colours, the villages, the towns and the city where I live.

The runs—and their stories—all head off from a light blue door which needs a more forceful yank shut when swollen by Autumn dampness. In the earliest days, I had programmed a sequence of directions to follow but this plan quickly evaporated, leaving behind as residue only the commitment to always cross the boundary of the local National Park. A backdrop of residential streets from different architectural periods follows the first measure of any run, a backdrop that thins away through the city's fringe into a series of staged territories which hover between town and country: parks, allotments, a golf course, wildflower-lined cinder paths, urban woods and expanses of grassland.

The debris of hubcaps, drink cans, cigarette packets and cigarette butts, paperboard clamshells with fading logos, glass bottles, plastic bottles, frayed rope, pallets and crutches, escapee flowers and vinyl gloves is always at its densest at the city's margins and its most dislocating when found at the outer radius of a run (the ugly weight of a black plastic bag spinning on a hawthorn bush). After a long time out on the hills, part of what it means to return is a fresh appreciation of the effects of exhaust on eyes, nostrils, mouth and ears, but any sense of the Downs' remoteness is always going to be relative in so thoroughly altered a landscape. On a winter's run along the crest, for example, a half hour might go by without seeing anyone else but there will still be contrails behind rending jets and still the laid-out shapes and textures of industrial agriculture, there will be clusters of light shining below, a building will cast an awkward geometry half-hidden behind branches and there will be patterns formed from electricity and telephone cables, fences, mobile masts, pylons and the paths we take and those we do not. This palm-on-palm clasp of rural and urban here in the South bubbled to the surface on New Year's Day when I walked with my wife to the out-of-time-copse. As we rounded the trail high above the copse, the winter's sun sent elongated shadows out from the copse's trees to reveal a sudden, perceptibly planted regularity that left much of the beauty I had always enjoyed there intact but at the same time dispelled at least part of my phantasy that this spot lay some way outside of human histories.

If there is a remoteness revealed by my runs, it comes before and after the light of the day. In the darkness, even the small urban wood that is 500 metres away from my light blue door becomes distant, disorientating, liable to spook.

If the out-of-time copse, the valley bowl and the numbered dew-ponds are my own coinings, some of the real names attached to the slopes, ridges and clefts that form the crease of the South Downs are printed across contour lines and come trailing Brows and Banks and Bottoms and Downs (of course) with Deans (or Denes), Hills and Coombes, Pits and Banks and—nearer the coast—Meres and Levels and Heads. There are features whose names would sink unnoticed into those thickly-inked maps printed after the title pages of *interbellum* adventure stories: the Meon, the Adur, the Arun, the Ouse and the Cuckmere, the Great Woods, Mount Caburn, Chanctonbury Ring, Blackcap, Wild Park, Scary Path, Devil's Dyke, Crooked Moon, Summer Down, Lower Rise, Upper Rise, High Hill, The Bostle.

A map like the one I have just crackled open holds the land and the names together, a flattened scale model where everything fits into its proper paper place. But what is fixed on the map with clean graphic neatness tends, when met on the ground, to come unstuck: the Downs that pressed through the soles of my feet felt there more as parts than they ever did as any greater sum. This experience of a partitioning led to those moments where my legs stopped, my ribs pressed outwards and then relaxed, my breath plumed in the cold air and I sought with my eyes and memory to connect the tufted field in front of me to the white tower blocks next to my children's former junior school or to plug the fizzing pylon into the single-street village that must be in the valley below.

The squat topography of the Downs may well be lidded by skylines that are seldom troubled by trees and may make panoramas of the north and the south, but the low elevations of the hills, their rolling profile and twisting paths mean that the uplands (such that they are) rarely turn a vantage on themselves and this deepens the feeling of a separated land of parts. If the clouds are high and the light is strong, then there are places to pause, swivel your head and take in the long, stretching escarpments or the next rising mass jutting out like a headland for a vanished sea. Yet what I have often encountered is less a connected world unfolded as vista and more a scrunched-up disjointed terrain, even after eighteen months of running. Consequently: the jolt of realisation that there is a well-trodden route from Wild Park up to the first dewpond by means of the old ski slope; the surprise to discover that by turning right at the fork in the path beyond the out-of-time copse you eventually get to the gurgling fulmars of the chalk cliffs; the disconnect when the white stables that I am expecting to see over the crown of close-cropped grass are still two undulating miles further on.

The sensory splintering of the Downs may be a condition of its compressed geology yet it also derives from the way I run and the ways in which that running is recorded. Once the programme of routes had been abandoned, a run initially involved time available being divided by distance possible; this meant that routes became modules, loops that once figured could be reconfigured in different combinations. In the earliest months of running, halting bile-throated and head hanging with hands on hips, the main routine was the 2 mile perimeter of the local urban wood not far from the end of my street. Then the repertoire extended: to the dual carriageway and back, 4 miles; from the dual carriageway through the flint wall and then round the old estate, 5 more miles; from the dual carriageway to the Beacon, 3 miles out and 3 miles return; from the Beacon to Blackcap, a 2 mile stretch east or, heading west, past the gate with blue farm twine, for 3.5 miles until Devil's Dyke; from the Dyke out to the witches' circle at Chanctonbury, 6 miles more. As I began to enter more arduous races—and as what had been casual runs became instrumentalised—the previous relationship between time and distance was flipped upside down. Instead of the availability of time determining which combination of modules would be chosen for a particular morning, afternoon or evening, brute distance came to reign supreme with time (and other obligations) having to fall into line behind.

Once I leave the pavements, my shoulders will relax, my face will angle forward and my gaze will shuttle between the ground with its protruding flints and tree roots and the immediate tunnel of vision ahead, a posture which splits me further from a view of a connected Downs. I'll watch my feet falling and read the shapes my hands have chosen for themselves. I'll glance down and catch claws and clenched fists, rigid martial arts palms, the sign of the horned devil, thumbs rubbing forefingers as connoisseur, thumbs protruding obscenely between finger joints, thumbs forming into a diver's OK or a hitchhiker's appeal, I'll spot crooked Vs and a delicate raised pinky.

The fragmentation created by this oscillating visual focus is compounded by parallel fluctuations in levels of conscious consciousness when I am running. As one leg stretches in front of another, my attention flickers between the throb of acute corporeal alertness, the drifts into vacancy that are only ever noticed in retrospect and the distraction of a mind so populated by inner verbalisations that sensations of movement, balance, heat, soreness and exertion are crowded out. The first run that I turned into writing was on a holiday far from the Downs:

> The heat already on the rise in the early morning, the moisture in the air and in the narrow channels to either side of the path, the smells coming off the vegetation still wet from last night's downpour; all these set a stage on which sense-memories of childhood visits to botanic gardens could play. A single cicada rubbed itself into hearing somewhere off to the right; as I ran past, my ears held onto the sound like a boat pulled taught against its anchor. On the way back, little spinning sounds as my footfalls disturbed lizards drying in the sun.

That this text shares the shuttering pulse that is common across the hundred stories collected in *A Downland Index* suggests that the episodic style has less to do with the specific qualities of the topography in East and West Sussex or a modular approach to distance and shifts the balance towards those other explanations of fragmentation such as my posture and the flickering between "eyes front" and "eyes down" or the fluctuations in consciousness.

Experiments with using a Dictaphone felt clumsy and trials with paper and pencil were even more awkward so any details that were collected on my runs ended up having to be carried along as thoughts—mulled over, honed sharper, dulled at their edges, consciously set aside or simply forgotten—until I arrived at the end with whatever had not drained away, with single words, place names, phrases, doodles, a connection; with yet more fragments. Anything that was perceived as new seemed to have a better chance of surviving the journey onto my notepad and yet, by the same token, other material persisted because it amounted to a repetition of something that had happened on an earlier jog.

From the initial rough notes, each run was documented in a format which I first used for Einar Hansen's *The Fog Will Clear The Snow Will Melt*. This format sets a text's length to one hundred words without imposing any stylistic influence: the writing can be staccato, it can flow or be simply a list of words; it can have an internal tone or it can observe what is outside; it is adaptable to talks, book chapters, exhibition catalogues. As a peculiar form of incentive, as soon as the texts were written I published them on an obscure Tumblr account.

I understand that the list is not exhaustive and know that a lot is missing. There is nothing in the book of fluffy clematis seed heads or mole hills, of the scut of a rabbit disappearing into dry thistles, of the fifth, sixth or seventh dewponds, of catkins, perimeters of fur, crocuses, kebab shops, hairdressers, traffic lights, drains, road markings, pizza takeaways, bus shelters, sheep's wool on barbed wire, of the birds I couldn't identify, of the incidents more embarrassing than ill-fitting shorts, sunburn, clothes pegs, caustic wolf whistles and other jokes at my expense.

Perhaps the most important part of running out on the Downs is muted in the book. In its pages there is only a meagre sense of collective agency, the occasional reference to 'we', 'our' or 'us' and the sporadic appearance of names that are anonymised to their initial letters. Though our conversations are as buried as the comfort of our silences, this layer of friendship, established or prospective, as much as "the beauty up here"—that is announced in the first story and then repeated eighteen months later in the last—is what these city streets, Downland hills and the hundred journeys along them came to offer me.